FAMILY CHRONICLE

FAMILY CHRONICLE

Poems and Photographs
of the Canadian West

James M. Moir

Gage Publishing
Toronto, Vancouver, Calgary, Montreal

Design by Mario Carvajal.

1   2   3   4   5   6   JD   4   3   2   1   0   9

Printed and bound in Canada.

Canadian Cataloguing in Publication Data

Moir, James M., 1914–
   Family chronicle

Poems.
ISBN 0–7715–9465–8 pa.

I. Title.

PS8576.O36F35   C811'.5'4   C78–001411–1
PR9199.3.M595F35

To my wife, in love and gratitude
and to Chris Wiseman, poet and friend.

The following poems have appeared before in these publications:

"When My People Came" – *Heritage* magazine
"Aunt Jen" – *Dandelion* magazine
"Ranch Wife" – *Spirit of Canada*
"Cattle-Buyers" – *Grain* magazine
"At the Rodeo" – *Heritage* magazine
"The Way My Cousin Tells It" – *Spirit of Canada* and *Heritage* magazine
"Mid-Winter Thaw" – *The Western Producer* and *Heritage*
"In the Hayfield" – *Grain* magazine
"The Abandoned Farm" – *Alberta Poetry Year Book*
"The Cricket" – *The Western Producer* magazine
"When the Bullying Wind Came" – *Dandelion* magazine
"A Young Farmer" – *Around You*
"Haying in the Old Days" – *The Western Producer* and *Heritage*
"An Indian Funeral" – *Alberta Poetry Year Book*
"The Ordeal" – *Hints 'N' Prods* magazine
"On Her Canvas" – *Canadian Author & Bookman* magazine
"The Politician's Grace" – *Hints 'N' Prods* magazine
"To-Day" – *Repository* magazine
"He Came Last Fall" – *Repository* magazine
"July Like a Clown" – *Foothills Review* magazine
"Joe Quesnel" – *Interface Tu* magazine

CONTENTS

OLD GEORGE

When I rode past his farm that afternoon
Old George was digging the potato crop.
The autumn sun shone warmly on his back
As he stooped down, and that must have been pleasant
Even to one as stoical as he,
Though he hardly paused to note the changing leaves
Or that the hills were tawny-colored now.
There were shadow-patterns under the yellowing trees,
A few clouds hung along the far horizon,
A magpie's croak had comic overtones.
What did it mean to George? Did he accept it
As animals accept the seasons' changes?
Knowing old George, I guessed what he was thinking;
Work must be done, and seasons come and go,
And whether he disliked it or he didn't
Had little to do with facts. Talk all you like;
Talk never changed life's facts one particle.
Once George was young, it's true, and had ideas;
Now the cocksure youth was gone, and what was left
Was a battered hat, a ragged grey mustache
And a lined face set in the mold of patience.
Jogging down the road I could plainly see
The days, like hounds, come harrying everyone
From the bright blossoming meadows of illusion.

THE MORNING WAS STILL

The morning was still
And I was alone
Brooding in the silence
When here he came
A big man perched
On an old white mare
His grey hair flying
And his eyes like flame.

Out of the fog
He came, he came
Riding on a cloud
In the late fall day.
"I've been talking
To God," he shouted.
"Soon we'll be seeing
That Judgement Day."

"A thin yield of wheat
And God's great bounty;
An empty house before me
And a barren field behind.
The road may be long
But my cares are taken
By the God that cures
The lame and the blind.

"Praise the Lord—
(O the good church meeting!)
Praise the Lord—
(O the young widow there!)
Praise the Lord—
(It will soon be Sunday!)"
—and his words faded out
in the dark autumn air.

JOE WAS NO FARMER

Joe was no farmer. He would rather talk
    And joke than work. Most work was just too hard.
He'd rather lounge than hoist himself and walk,
    And time—why he could waste it by the yard.
His friend, big-hearted Tommy, lived nearby
    And helped him till Joe's missus felt ashamed.
"Is it a crime" Tom asked, "to like the guy?
    If that's my reason, how can I be blamed?"

"Sometimes I think I shouldn't have come west.
    "For two cents I would leave," snapped Mrs. Joe.
Joe only laughed. A neighbor, unimpressed,
    Said, "Well then, if that's all you need to go
I've got two cents. Here, take it if you will."
She looked as though for two cents she could kill.

THE ORDEAL

His voice
was a wind
that swept my thoughts aside;
a torrent that
drowned me.

His raucous laugh
drew me down
into a mire
of ignorance.

He tossed back
a few last words;
they clung
like burrs.

From the great plain
of his presumption
I retreat
to my half-acre
of defiance.

WHEN MY PEOPLE CAME

When my people came to the hills
they built a log cabin
beside trees and running water
in a silent lonely place;
all they heard
was the chirr of the cricket
and a few bird-songs.

The grass was tall
and the cattle fattened;
the rain came
and it seemed a land of plenty.
They had not seen the lean shadows
of the summer drought
or the long winter.

Who can repeat the story
of those days
not having known them?
The sun was a towering July giant
that December lost
in the blizzard's white confusion.
After the storm, they looked out
on a stark landscape
gripped by bitter frost.

Seared by ice and fire,
it was a land of fierce
and stubborn energy
that slowly softened into

the grass and flowers of spring.
Cattle moved out to pasture,
larks sang and crocuses
blossomed on sunny knolls.

The huge hill-solitude
was home.

THE OLD MAN

The rain came in the night
and the old man turned his head to hear.
"Maybe it will rain to-morrow," he thought.

The next morning the rain still fell
on the little shack among the trees
and, grateful, he lay long in his bed.
When he arose, he ate a few scraps of food,
and lay long again,
glad of the respite from work,
his thoughts of a past
when life was wide and vivid
and not yet diminished
to the measurements of a lonely farm.

And the swirl of the storm-clouds passed overhead.

There was a musty smell in the shack
and the room was airless.
Old clothes were there and trivia from the past.
Sometimes there were faces and voices;
shadows of those who had been the props of his life.
Now life was roofless under the winds of change.

Here was no easy balance leading to a happy conclusion;
here was a wavering retreat to death.

The rain ending left him with silence
and the impassive trees and hills.

THE WAY MY COUSIN TELLS IT

The way my cousin
tells it
it's back in 1935;
he's out in the field
puttin' in his crop.
Times are tough,
prices are low,
dust's a-flyin',
there's no rain
this year or last
and his debts get bigger
all the time.
On top of all that
a meadowlark singin'
sounds like
"You'll go broke!
you'll go broke!"

My cousin
pulls up his horses
and yells right back.
"DAMN it all, bird,
watch your language."

BEDINGTON AND BROWN

Tom Bedington was a pagan, I admit;
 A happy sinner, cool and debonair
And this, being added to his ribald wit,
 Made Paul Brown shake his head in grim despair.

He tried exhorting Bedington, to see
 If he could turn him from his evil ways.
(Paul Brown was earnest to the Nth degree
 And sternly duty-bound through all his days.)
"Whiskey I never touch," said pious Brown.
 "Neither do I. I drink it," said his friend.
"That dreadful whorehouse at the edge of town,"
 Hissed Paul, "I hate to pass it."
          "I contend
One shouldn't," said the other with a grin.
"When I'm down there I always wander in."

THE BLACK SHEEP

She was a big woman;
her shadow
under the sun
bulked large
but not so large
as the intangible shadow
of worry
that followed her.

To-day
all her movements
expressed agitation;

no consolation of words
could change her.

She turned
to her visitor.
"Dat boy," she sighed,
"dat boy.
Pokers all his money away."

AN INDIAN FUNERAL

(After seeing the Peter Whyte painting at Banff)

The chief is brought to his last resting-place;
The feelings of the tribe gather on the snowy hill.
Death brings no wampum; they must bring wampum to Death.
Many faces are inscrutable; some show grief.
He was their father.
He was the vessel containing wisdom and strength.
Now that the vessel is broken their thirst rises.
They call in their hearts for a father
But he was their last father.
Now they must find their lonely way
Through a barren white world.

THE ABANDONED FARM

The sagging fence
serves no purpose;
the empty foundation
stares at the sky.

Rabbit and owl
inhabit the woodlot.

An old wagon
half buried in snow
is abandoned like this farm
and forgotten.

Trees
stand out darkly
then like memories
are half-obscured
by drifting fog.

Silence
holds the hour
in a white twilight.

To-day
the forgotten farm
knows only
a cold harvest of snow.

MID-WINTER THAW

I

Earth smiles again, for she is sun-caressed;
   A chickadee calls gaily from his tree
   Watching with perky curiosity
As Jim splits wood, stript to his shirt and vest.
A neighbor rides along beside the fence
   And stops to visit. By the barn's red wall
   The cows look on, too lazy even to bawl;
The barnyard is a haven of indolence.

"Who do you think got married yesterday?
   And what's old Charley's latest, have you heard?"
The magpie in the trees, a step away,
   Turns an inquisitive head, the nosey bird,
Listening to the neighbors gossiping
And hoping that the sun means it is spring.

II

There is a steady dripping from the eaves;
   Old Chub, the saddle horse, stands by the gate
   Too sleepy to do anything but wait
And dream of glorious banquets of oat-sheaves.
A deer is silhouetted by the creek,
   A porcupine is hunched in a willow-tree;
   The sun has put us in a trance, I see,
And we shall not be normal for a week.

All through the afternoon the sun will shine
  With shadows patterned blue on gleaming white,
And grateful birds in our back yard shall dine
  While the cat, sun-soaked, dozes full in sight.
There's nothing behaving as it used to do
Now this warm sudden day has broken through.

CATTLE-BUYERS

the boy stands shyly
    watches and listens
strange men have come
    to his father's ranch
to look at
    it may be to buy
        cattle
in the shadow of
    the cottonwoods
        that breathe sleep
they talk   light cigarettes
    break wind
        bark with laughter
big men breathing
    strength and money
he listens   wonders
    about their world
what is it like
    what do they do
        in that unknown place
beyond this lost corner
    this lonely range
where the sun
    holds the hills
        in a lariat of heat

AUNT JEN

Aunt Jen treated churches
with scorn;
they could all keep
their wings and their harps.
The way they bawled hymns
made her laugh.
Besides, how could you fly
up there
with no atmosphere
to support you?
Once only
she had a short encounter
with God
when an illness
sent her helpless to bed
and she made the family
play hymns
over and over
on the phonograph
until she recovered.

BEREAVEMENT

When the tractor
came into old George's life
he danced attendance on her
continually.
His hand on her fender
was a lover's caress;
he spoke of her
with fire in his eye
and his "putt-putt-chuck-chuck"
imitation of her voice
as she turned over
the blanket of a furrow
was full of love.

The day the machine company
repossessed her
he stood staring
at a Russian thistle
that held out dry barbs
in front of him.

When a cricket
in the hot noon
said, "Weep, weep,"
he went indoors
and collapsed on his bed.
For two days
he lay there
at grief's level
his face to the wall.

PAT HARRIGAN

Pat Harrigan was Irish born and bred;
    Wherever there was fighting to be found
Pat would be represented at its head
    Slugging until his foes were on the ground.
Pat was a giant, strong as a dozen men.
    Talking to him, you chose your words with care;
And if he had been on the booze, why then
    Strong men turned pale, and women turned to prayer.

One time he made a man get on his knees
And eat grass like a horse, and then say, "please";
    There was no deviltry he wouldn't do.
Yet when we finally met, he shook my hand
And said, "Was John your father? He was grand;
    The finest gentleman I ever knew."

FROM HIS FARMHOUSE WINDOW

From his farmhouse window
we watched the sunset.

When he spoke
his expression changed.

"In this country," he told me
"you can't look at a sunset
without wondering
about the weather.

When I first came here
it seemed all they talked about
was bushels and acreage.
Lately I notice
that's all I talk about myself."

(Just as he spoke
a stormy sky
threatened our crops
with hail.)

THE WAY IT LOOKED TO HIM

"Come on and have a drink of beer with me,"
Big Charley said when I arrived in town.
Though Charley seemed a man of the world to me
I was young and green and just a little scared
Of alcohol (my folks had warned me of it)
And so I answered, "Sure, I'll come along
But I won't drink."

      "Then you're not much like Ralph,"
Said Charley with a twinkle in his eye.
"I invited *him* to come an hour ago.
Guess what he told me.

      'Yeah, I wouldn't mind
But if I'm seen in the beer parlor with you
Then people will be saying that I drink.'
'Look Ralph,' (I should have said) 'come up to the house.
It's dark in the cellar and we'll have one there.'"

IN THE HAYFIELD

The boy's resentment
was like the sultry heat.

His mower
clashed defiance.

Baffled,
his father looked,
then looked away.

The day
altered its course.
It moved among clouds
and the wind
began to whip away
the prairie wool
as they mowed.

The wind
in the fence-wires
sang of escape.

The boy listened.

Glaring upward,
the older man
cursed the weather
and the storm shook
a fist of lightning
overhead.

A YOUNG FARMER

The days stretch out
endless with toil.

The hard land
thrusts him along
his inevitable way.

Enclosed in lonely spaces
of earth and sky
he seeks his to-morrow.

With darkness in his blood
he lies in darkness
at the day's end,

hearing the wind sigh
over miles of prairie.

THE POLITICIAN'S GRACE

The politician's grace
   I scarcely could believe;
"May the Lord make us thankful
   for those we shall deceive."

TO-DAY

Last night
   I had too much
      I had much too much
         to drink

I know
   that God does not mark
      the sparrow's fall
         to-day

To-day
   he has turned
      his whole attention
         toward me
(O God
   why must I
      be so
         noticeable?)

If ever I face
   the world again
      this shall be
         said of me

"Behold!
   a camel that stares
      into a needle's
         eye."

FAMILY CHRONICLE

The old log house knew us.
Grandfather with his pipe and his one dram too many;
grandmother with her patience and her knitting;
uncle Arnold who could not endure her death
and was found weeping under the poplars;
mother, who cooked for a house full of people
and was resentful;
and that brash girl
who teased the lame hired man
until he arose, roaring,
and chased her through the door.
Unheeding in the next room
grandfather, grown dram-drowsy,
toppled into bed, his snore
raucous with rum.

The old house saw uncle Arnold, grey-headed now,
forget work for a whole Sunday
and turn to the newspaper,
made virtuous by the knowledge
of a full granary and a huge woodpile,
father meanwhile dispensing
geniality like sunlight—
tolerant (apparently) toward the whole world—
and glad too that uncle Arnold
would stay on and work.

And what if that household
were here to-day
confronted by the enigma
that is the last of us?
It is whispered that he is a poet,
a sworn enemy of work
and drunk on his own words.
O what would they say?

HE CAME LAST FALL

He came last fall.
All winter we used to see him
hanging around the pool-room,
sitting in the beer-parlor,
grinning,
telling stories through cigarette-smoke,
talking cars, talking dances,
talking girls,
shovelling BS,
occasionally shovelling snow for the folks,
helping at the service station,
getting tipsy on dance-nights,
forgetting the whole shooting-match
at the dance;
I guess it was good enough
while it lasted.

One day
tired of little jobs
and the two-bit ways
of a prairie town,
he looked up at the spring sky
and just like that
the April wind had him
and he was gone
to the gulls and the girls
and the big-time deals
in Vancouver.

HAYING IN THE OLD DAYS

The summer morning said to us,
"This is the day for haying."

Yesterday the long preparation;
to-day the conquest.

The sun was there before us
high in his own hayfield

tossing down
great forkfuls of sunlight.

Our nodding horses
moved up and down the rows
of toppling grass.

The fragrance of mowed hay
arose on the air.

A lark
threw ringing circles of song
into the green rectangle of meadow.

The slow current of afternoon
moved toward the silver cataract
of evening.

Shadows were giants
fallen on the ground
when our wagons clacked home.

WHEN THE BULLYING WIND CAME

When the bullying wind came
he seized the hills in his arms
and they wrestled;
all day long
the wind roared and tumbled
through the country
                of the hills.

But the hills are mighty;
they have the strength
of their immensity,
and it was the wind that night
the beaten wind
                who fell back.

RAINY DAY AT DAVIS CREEK

This morning
for the third day
grey birds of storm
hang overhead.
Indoors, a warm house
and soggy boots
by the fire
but beyond the window
trees drip
stacks are sodden-topped
and cows hunch their backs
in the wet.
The creek
is a roaring, drunken
giant.
Picking her way
through the mud
the grey pony carries me
up the valley
to Bill's place.
Walrus moustache
and Scottish burr,
he meets me at the door.
"What's the weather report?"
I ask.
"Last night
our radio quit."
Bill
veteran of hill-life
grins

and answers
"Well, it's Tuesday to-morry
— if it doesna rain."

He steps back.
"Come awa' " he says,
"come awa' ben.
Bad weather
means good talk."

JERRY

It was threshing-time.
He wasn't even
boss of the outfit
but he jumped on my rack
to tell me off about
some knot-headed thing
that didn't amount to
a hill of beans
and he wouldn't stop.
That was Jerry—
half moron and half bully,
his brain a cracked mirror
distorting the world.
I was young and green
and that kind of nonsense
didn't come easy
but I gave it a good try.
"Damn you," I said,
"If you don't get the hell
off my bundle-rack
and shut up
I'm gonna shove my fork
right through you."
He hesitated
but finally
            grudgingly
he did.
I suppose you could say
it was practice
for tougher roles in life

but I didn't thank him
for the rehearsal.
Instead, I described for him
seventeen varieties of
stupid, ornery coyote,
named him first among them
and drove off.

FOR AN OLD FRIEND

On a dark afternoon
we talked of him,
we who had known him so long.
(The day that he died
was a dark day
at the end of the year.)

I spoke of the time
that I met him;
I remembered his words.
(I spoke of him quietly.
He was a quiet man.)

The narrow ways of age
were never his;
he walked again
through the fields of youth
as he talked.
(I spoke of him gently
for he was gentle.)

Silently we clasped hands,
we who had known him,
and as I turned at the door,
the brooding clouds,
falling at last
under their own burden,
released the snow.

ON HER CANVAS

she sits at her canvas
a whole country world
before her

the sullen bull
glares from his pasture

a weasel peers fiercely
from a rock-pile

a hawk strikes
at a sparrow

the sun
is a mountain-lion

he rakes the land
with burning claws

on her canvas
is a water-lily
in a pond

RANCH WIFE

All day she has followed
the solitary road
of her work and her thoughts
and now in the early evening
she opens the door
and looks out to the west
where low sun touches grass-tops
on the far side of the valley.
In the distance, a rider
moves across tawny fields.
A saddle horse, alone in the pasture,
flings up his head
and sends out a wild whinny
across the hills
as he sees loaded hay-wagons
coming toward home.
A crow flaps heavily away
and there is a feeling in the air
that summer is fading
and change is near.
The woman's eyes brood.
She dreams of an English past;
she dreads the long winter
which shall imprison her.
The veery, that lost spirit,
calls from the trees.
Night, like a great river,
flows through the hills.

SO THIS IS YOUR LITTLE TOWN

So this is your little town.
No one here
but the four-square businessman,
the giggling teenager, the retired farmer,
and drunken Andy down the way.
Nothing here but two general stores,
a service station,
a beer parlor and a rink.
Once you were a big name at the rodeos;
cheered by the crowds;
a top hand from the Bar-X.
Now that you have come to this,
how do you live through the hot days
in your little house
with the lonely sound
of a newspaper by the window
rustling in the wind
and a parched poplar
complaining at your door?

Out on the ranches they are haying now.

How do you live through the days
when winter, the hunter
with a rifle of frost,
crouches in ambush outside?

When you were young
you rode the broncho of life
like the cowboy you were.
Now that you have been
thrown from the saddle,
how can you live at all?

JULY LIKE A CLOWN

Surrounded by flowers
the slow clocks of the season
I sit in the silence

idly attempting to translate
the words of a wren
in the apple-tree

when July like a clown
in a spangled costume
comes bouncing in

bringing herds of tourists,
runaway cars,
backyard radios,

trampled lawns,
jangling doorbells
and jangled nerves.

But bringing also
in lovely contrast
that happy season

when girls in bikinis
lie in ambush
on the beaches

and young men are brought down
like sitting ducks
by the shotgun of love.

THE CRICKET

The cricket tries to be heard.
Old habits die hard.
"Whee," he says, "whee, whee"
but the cars speed by
unheeding.

Years ago
people drove into these hills
with horses,
and heard the sound of the cricket;
heard him
all a summer's day;

And the cricket trilled on
charmed
by his own song.
"Repeat," he told his brothers,
"repeat, repeat."

JOE QUESNEL

I
Joe Quesnel
          dustbowl farmer
patched blue denims
                    and leather face
stands at the edge
                of his wheatfield.
Nothing there
            but shrivelled stalks
and Russian thistle—
                    legacies of heat.
Sun over prairie
                dances a devil's dance
thrusts steel-hot fingers
into grass to its roots.
No living earth this;
only dry bones.

II
Confused voices   a river of sound
faces that change
                    into other faces
glasses of beer on the table
a last barricade
                against to-day.
Leaving his chair
he performs a slow ballet
movements at all angles
movements
            that bring him
            to the street.

"Alec," he calls
                "Hey Alec"
and a man turns.
With cowboy yells
they grab each other
and Joe's hat
                falls to the ground.
He reaches down   holds it up;
bystanders see
a sprig of Russian thistle
tucked in its ribbon.
"Damn" he sneers
"Damn flower
                o' S'katchewan"
and growling
                they reel away.

TOM McGEE

"I've worked all week on a blasted rocky farm
And if I feel like comin' into town
For a few beers with the boys, by God I'll do it."
(Tom McGee was talking to his conscience.)
I told him, "Tom, work when you bloody work,
Play when you bloody play. Forget the rest."
But that was not McGee.
                        And he continued
"I pay my taxes and I pay my bills
And I'm as good as any man there is."

After two bottles, I could see him thawing.
"Old man Pilsner's doin' fine to-day;
I'll stay a little longer," (and he grinned).
So I said, "See you later," and left town.
Next day, I took the mare out for a canter.
It was one of those first-class days of early fall;
Even the beat-up grass looked good to me.
When I rode past McGee's I was surprised
To see him out repairing his cattle-shed.
"Tom, why in hell do you have to work on Sunday?"
His eyes were red and he squinted in the sun.
"Guys that go and get drunk on Saturday night
Need a good kick in the ass by Sunday," says he.

WHEN WINTER COMES

When winter comes we have the antidote
    With hot rum punch beside a roaring fire
    And contests to see who's the biggest liar
Or who can sing the very lowest note,
And dances every Friday (my o my!)
    With all the pretty girls you'd care to see
    While the old folks say "That boy looks wild to me.
I hope he never gives *our* girl the eye."

Alf plays the banjo, Ben the violin;
    We dance for hours and still we ask for more.
When my watch says half-past three we pack it in
    And pull up at the ranch again by four;
The frosty runners squeaking on our sleigh,
Our hungry cattle bawling for their hay.

BERT DANIELS

Bert Daniels said strange things, no one knew why;
　　He must have been a trial to poor Belle.
He found it hard to look you in the eye
　　But in the field of insolence did well.
He could sit talking with you for an hour
　　And even show some slight humanity,
Then in a twinkling he'd begin to sour
　　And make a bitter comment. Such was he.

He ate a meal with Joe and Lizzie Benn
　　Bowing his ornery head as she said grace,
Talked casually of this and that, and then
　　Snarled suddenly, with a dark look on his face
"Don't ever let me catch you two again
　　Stealing the saskatoons from Daniels' place."

AT THE RODEO

He settles himself
in the saddle
pulls down his hat
looks up and nods.
The gate is opened
and they plunge
into the arena.
Tossed and jerked
by the thrust
of the broncho's
powerful body
the cowboy
with deceptive ease
rides the whirlwind.
The crowd roars its praise.

Old Tom
once a top rider
is silent now
among the cheering voices
cigarette smoke
like memories
around his head.
Dazed and battered
he stands alone
riding
      still riding.

EPITAPH FOR THE PIONEERS

The drama of their lives
Was played before the backdrop of the hills,
And before the backdrop of the hills
Their lives ended.

The brilliant sun lighted their ways,
The dark winter storms waylaid them;
Now, both courage and fear forgotten,
All with them is darkness.

Who shall recover the truth of their days?
What can reveal it?
Not the hawk wheeling in the sky
Nor the distant blue hills,
Nor the enquiring dreamer
Who comes to their graves.